DIFFERENT BUT EQUAL

APPRECIATING DIVERSITY

CAITIE MCANENEY

PowerKiDS press™

NEW YORK

Published in 2020 by The Rosen Publishing Group, Inc.
29 East 21st Street, New York, NY 10010

Editor: Elizabeth Krajnik
Designer: Michael Flynn

Photo Credits: Cover LWA/DigitalVision/Getty Images; cover, pp. 1, 3–4, 6, 8–10, 12, 14–16, 18, 20–24 (background) TairA/Shutterstock.com; p. 4 marekuliasz/Shutterstock.com; p. 5 Brocreative/Shutterstock.com; p. 6 Anton Bielousov/Shutterstock.com; p. 7 ESB Professional/Shutterstock.com; p. 9 Eleanor Bentall/Corbis Historical/Getty Images; p. 10 Matthias Hangst/Getty Images Sport/Getty Images; p. 11 Joseph Sohm/Shutterstock.com; p. 13 (top) Steve Heap/Shutterstock.com; p. 13 (bottom) https://commons.wikimedia.org/wiki/File:Civil_Rights_March_ on_Washington,_D.C._(Dr._Martin_Luther_King,_Jr._speaking.)_-_NARA_-_542068.tif; p. 15 Thomas Barwick/DigitalVision/Getty Images; p. 16 https://commons.wikimedia.org/wiki/File:Frida_Kahlo,_by_Guillermo_Kahlo.jpg; p. 17 MIGUEL MEDINA/AFP/Getty Images; p. 19 Dmytro Zinkevych/Shutterstock.com; p. 20 Helioscribe/Shutterstock.com; p. 21 Sandor Szmutko/Shutterstock.com; p. 22 Rawpixel.com/Shutterstock.com.

Library of Congress Cataloging-in-Publication Data

Names: McAneney, Caitie, author.
Title: Different but equal : appreciating diversity / Caitie McAneney.
Description: New York : PowerKids Press, [2020] | Series: Spotlight on social
  and emotional learning | Includes index.
Identifiers: LCCN 2018059161| ISBN 9781725306691 (pbk.) | ISBN 9781725306721
  (library bound) | ISBN 9781725306707 (6 pack)
Subjects: LCSH: Cultural pluralism--Juvenile literature. |
  Multiculturalism--Juvenile literature. | Toleration--Juvenile literature.
Classification: LCC HM1271 .M385 2020 | DDC 305.8--dc23
LC record available at https://lccn.loc.gov/2018059161

Manufactured in the United States of America

CPSIA Compliance Information: Batch #CWPK20. For further information contact Rosen Publishing, New York, New York at 1-800-237-9932.

CONTENTS

CHAPTER ONE

A DIVERSE WORLD

The world is a diverse place! When something is diverse, it means that thing is made up of people or things that are different from each other. On Earth, there are many different kinds of landscapes, animals, plants, and people.

People come in all shapes, sizes, and colors. They speak different languages, live in different parts of the world, have different **customs**, eat different foods, and come from different family situations. Even though all people are different, that doesn't mean they can't get along. In fact, it's important to appreciate, or be grateful for, and celebrate the diversity in our world!

Look around your classroom. How are people different? How are they the same? How can you celebrate people's differences instead of disliking and complaining about them? Even though not everyone is just like you, all people deserve respect.

The United States of America is a cultural mosaic. This means that it's a **society** made up of different **cultures**.

CHAPTER TWO

SOCIAL AWARENESS

Appreciating diversity is part of social awareness. Social awareness is when someone has the ability to empathize with, or understand, others and think about things from their **perspective**. These other people include people who are different from you and who might come from a background or culture different from yours.

You can celebrate many parts of a culture, including that culture's dances.

Social awareness also includes the ability to understand and appreciate how people act and feel when they come from different backgrounds and cultures. Different cultures have different social and **ethical** norms, which are standards of proper or acceptable behavior. These norms may seem strange to you at first. However, if you exercise your social awareness, you'll probably learn something new! Above all, social awareness has to do with respecting others—no matter how different they may be.

CHAPTER THREE

WHAT ARE DIFFERENCES?

One of the first things people often notice about others is their appearance. People have different skin colors, hair colors, and eye colors. Sometimes, people with similar skin color and features are considered to be part of the same race.

People also have different abilities. Some people can walk easily, while others need to use wheelchairs. Some people learn easily, while others struggle to learn. Just because a person has a different ability doesn't mean they can't achieve their goals!

Everyone's background is different, too. Some people have a lot of money to spend, while others don't have much money at all. Some people live in big houses, while others live in small apartments. Some people live with a mom and dad, while others live with one parent, grandparents, foster parents, two moms, or two dads. Every family is different!

Stephen Hawking spent much of his life in a wheelchair, unable to speak on his own. However, he's one of the most famous scientists in history.

CHAPTER FOUR

THE BENEFITS OF DIVERSITY

Understanding the many benefits of diversity in your community will help you appreciate diversity more. Different kinds of people bring new ideas and opinions to a community. They may bring new skills, products, foods, and talents. These things help the **economy** grow.

The opening ceremony of the Olympics is a chance for the host country to showcase its culture, history, and successes.

BARACK OBAMA

CHANGE WE NEED

WWW.**BARACKOBAMA**.COM

Imagine a world in which everyone listened to the same music, wore the same clothes, ate the same foods, and did the same dances. This would probably be pretty boring! Having a diverse community can introduce people to new art forms, foods, fashions, and cultural knowledge. We can thank people from other countries for foods such as tamales and lasagna, for dances such as samba and tango, and for many different kinds of music.

Working to make our communities more diverse can help society become more fair and just. For example, Barack Obama's presidential **campaign** brought together people from many backgrounds, united in the idea that, together, we can do anything.

CHAPTER FIVE

SAY NO TO PREJUDICE

Prejudice is an opinion or set of opinions someone has about someone else that isn't based on facts. It's usually based on the person's idea of the other person's race, sex, background, abilities, or appearance. Sometimes people use prejudices as reasons to pay other people less, call them names, leave them out of jobs, or even hurt or kill them.

No one is born with prejudice. It's something that people learn as they grow up. They see how the people around them treat others unfairly or have unfair opinions, and sometimes they **develop** their own prejudices. One way to fight prejudice is to learn more about people who are different from you.

When you see someone treating another person unfairly, you can stand up for that other person. Martin Luther King Jr. fought against prejudice, especially racism. Racism is the belief that one group or race of people is better than another group or race.

Martin Luther King Jr. once said, "I have a dream that my four little children will one day live in a nation where they will not be judged by the color of their skin but by the content of their character."

MARTIN LUTHER KING JR. MEMORIAL
WASHINGTON, D.C.

CHAPTER SIX

BE RESPECTFUL

Being respectful of people who are different from you is a very important social skill. Having respect for someone includes how you feel about them and how you treat them. When you treat someone with respect, it means you show them that you care about their wellbeing and their feelings.

You can be respectful toward someone even if you don't agree with them. Sometimes people have different thoughts and opinions than you do. Some people have different religious beliefs and political opinions. Imagine that someone in your class thinks kids should go to school all year. But you think kids should have summer vacation. You can listen to the other person's opinion and disagree with them while still being respectful. People have their own beliefs and opinions for a reason. By listening to them, you might learn something new.

Being respectful of someone means not forming an opinion about them until you really get to know them.

CHAPTER SEVEN

LEARN ABOUT IT!

You might have heard the saying "Don't judge someone until you've walked a mile in their shoes." One of the best ways to walk in another person's shoes is to learn more about their culture or way of life.

How can you learn about someone's culture or way of life? Just ask! Many people are willing and happy to talk about their traditions, customs, and beliefs. Make sure you ask and listen with openness and acceptance.

You can also read books about different cultures or ways of life. You can read both fiction and nonfiction. Nonfiction books can teach you facts about the history, customs, and traditions of a group of people. Fiction books with main characters who are different from you can help you see things from a different perspective.

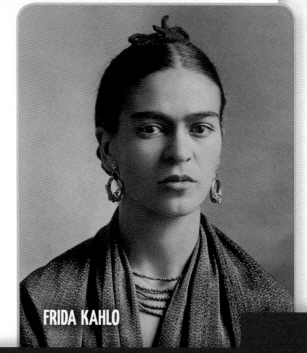

FRIDA KAHLO

You can learn a lot about a culture by looking at its art. Frida Kahlo was a famous Mexican painter known for her self-portraits.

CHAPTER EIGHT

GETTING INVOLVED

What if you don't know many people who are different from you? Some people live in communities made up of people who are mostly the same. That makes it hard to meet other kinds of people!

Getting involved in your community or another community is a great way to meet new people. You can **volunteer** to work at a soup kitchen to understand how people who have little money live. You can also help an elderly neighbor shovel their driveway or sidewalk and ask them questions to hear about their way of life.

If you volunteer or participate at a community center or charity event, or with a volunteer organization, you might meet lots of people who are different from you. You can learn a lot from these people! Getting outside of your comfort zone helps you grow and gain new perspectives.

Volunteering brings people together. Whether you're planting trees or collecting cans of food for a soup kitchen, you're working together to make a difference!

CHAPTER NINE

CELEBRATING DIVERSITY

How can you celebrate diversity in your community? Some communities have **international** festivals where you can try foods from around the world. International music festivals will have music from around the world.

The people pictured here are celebrating Puerto Rican **heritage**. At parades like this one, you can listen to music, eat **traditional** foods, and watch traditional dances.

   Some events, including some festivals and parades, celebrate one culture or way of life. Each year in June, many states have pride parades, which celebrate the **LGBTQ** community. Also in June, some African American communities celebrate the end of slavery with a Juneteenth parade. Some cities have parades to celebrate Irish heritage on Saint Patrick's Day. There's Irish music, food, and dancing! Check your local newspaper or your community's visitor website to see what kinds of festivals and parades take place in your community. You may be able to learn important things about other cultures or ways of life at these events.

A COMMUNITY QUILT

Some people have prejudices against people who are different from them. They want everyone to look and act like they do and have the same opinions and beliefs. Prejudice is very hurtful and can make people afraid to be their true selves around others.

It's important to remember that the United States is made up of many different kinds of people from all over the world. That's part of what makes the United States special! **Immigrants** came to the Americas and founded the United States, and the immigrants who come to this country today make it even more special.

Your community is like a patchwork quilt made up of cloths of different shapes and colors. Diversity makes your community strong and beautiful. When you appreciate and celebrate diversity, you become a part of the quilt.

GLOSSARY

campaign (kaam-PAYN) A plan to achieve a certain result.

culture (KUHL-chuhr) The beliefs and ways of life of a certain group of people.

custom (KUH-stuhm) An action or way of behaving that is traditional among the people in a certain group or place.

develop (dih-VEHL-uhp) To bring out the possibilities of, to begin to have gradually, or to create over time.

economy (ih-KAH-nuh-mee) The amount of buying and selling in a place.

ethical (EH-thuh-kuhl) Based on ethics, or rules based on what's right and what's wrong.

heritage (HEHR-uh-tihj) The traditions and beliefs that are part of the history of a group or nation.

immigrant (IH-muh-gruhnt) A person who comes to a country to live there.

international (ihn-tuhr-NASH-nuhl) Involving two or more countries.

LGBTQ (ell-gee-bee-tee-kew) An acronym that stands for lesbian, gay, bisexual, transgender, and queer. The term also applies to those whose gender or sexuality is outside of mainstream society.

perspective (puhr-SPEK-tihv) Point of view.

society (suh-SY-uh-tee) A community, nation, or broad grouping of people having common traditions, activities, and interests.

traditional (truh-DISH-nuhl) Following what's been done for a long time.

volunteer (vah-luhn-TEER) To do something to help because you want to do it.

INDEX

PRIMARY SOURCE LIST

Page 9
Professor Stephen Hawking, British theoretical physicist. Photograph. Eleanor Bentall. Centre for Mathematical Sciences, University of Cambridge, Great Britain. Now kept in the Corbis Historical collection on Getty Images.

Page 13
Martin Luther King Jr. at the March on Washington. Photograph. U.S. Information Agency. Press and Publications Service. August 28, 1963. Washington, D.C. Now kept at the National Archives at College Park.

Page 16
Frida Kahlo. Gelatin silver print photograph. Guillermo Kahlo. October 16, 1932.

WEBSITES

Due to the changing nature of Internet links, PowerKids Press has developed an online list of websites related to the subject of this book. This site is updated regularly. Please use this link to access the list: www.powerkidslinks.com/SSEL/diversity